The Female Cha

In 2023

CW00833055

Mario Novakovic

Spaces. intimate, personal, and enclosed. Open and vast. communicative and engaging. empowering and empowering. The idea of space and the word "space" encompass many other possibilities. Space is a crucial creative and compositional component in the visual arts, negotiating sculptural forms and arranging painted forms, tones, and light. For the artist, spatial palpability goes beyond mere convention; It gives the work a new lease on life. It gives meaning to that energy, that life-giving force, adding another layer of symbolism for the artist and the viewer.

In his book The Poetics of Space, the French writer and philosopher Gaston Bachelard investigates the fundamental response that people have to space. According to Bachelard, the actual spaces of our lives—our homes—are compartments of meaning that we keep in our memories and dreams and let go of when we respond to the world. In response, Michael Pollan makes the observation that Bachelard envisioned shelter or space as a necessary requirement for contemplation and creativity. He cites Bachelard's writing as saying, According to Pollan (7), "the house shelters daydreaming, the dreamer is protected, and one can dream peacefully in the house." Once more, I'd like to borrow a connection that Pollan makes between Bachelard's thoughts and Virginia Woolf's when she says that every woman writer should have her own room (7–8). Woolf asserts that space and creativity are particularly related to female writers. The female writer is given the freedom to pursue and record her thoughts when a private space is created and preserved.

According to Pollan, this "room of one's own" is a "modern invention," as suggested by contemporary authors like Woolf and Bachelard (8). Spatial Dynamics and Female Development in Victorian Art and Novels intrigued artists and writers of a slightly earlier period, the nineteenth century. This is partly due to emerging modern notions of the self as individual1 and modern, privatized arrangements of interior living spaces2. Despite this time specificity, the links between spaces and interiority seem strongly provocative.

On the off chance that the picture of a lady essayist's own room showed up so obviously and powerfully to

Virginia Woolf in the mid 20th 100 years, bits of that picture and investigations of that association might have proactively been surfacing during the Victorian time frame.

The project's direction is derived from these ideas. In a broader sense, I intend to investigate the similarities and differences that exist between Victorian women's novels and the visual and verbal aspects of Victorian art. Both forms communicate via visual and verbal/literal means, despite being separated by medium. More specifically, I want to investigate the use of spatial composition in the creation of female characters and figures. I will focus on the terms of what constitutes spatial composition by using vivid examples from male and female Victorian artists like Edward Burne-Jones, Elizabeth Siddall, Jessica Hayllar, Maria Spartali Stillman, Lord Frederick Leighton, Rebecca Solomon, Dante Gabriel Rossetti, John Everett Millais, and Augustus Egg's paintings and sketches of the female figure.

The various artistic movements of the time are represented by these mid-to-late 1800s artists: Academic Social, Aesthetic/Victorian Renaissance, and Pre-

Raphaelite Paintings The works that have been selected will visually place women in symbolic spatial compositions and dynamics that are comprehensible to us and the Victorian era. My research and questions aim to demonstrate how these dynamics are reflected in three particular Victorian novels written by women authors. I'm talking about these spaces—locations, enclosures, etc.—in my writing and novels. as a metaphor for social, cultural, and psychological internal conditions. Even though this research looks at the work of male and female artists, it only looks at women's novels. However, both genders' work may have provided reading spaces and alternative meanings during this time period.

A brief look at two paintings in which the spatial composition corresponds to the presentation and development of the female figure may be helpful. Two typologies are represented by these examples: one is a space for women only;

the other is a gender-interactive space. The Travelling Companions (1862) by academic and social painter Augustus Leopold Egg depicts two young women traveling together, probably as sisters or close friends because they are dressed identically.3 The young woman on the left side of the canvas is sleeping in her own private space with her drowsy head leaning toward the carriage's coast-viewing window. The woman on the right is also a representation of her own world because she is absorbed in her book. The passing scene outside her window does not appear to pique their interest, alertness, or influence. Instead, they appear content and absorbed in their respective private spaces and activities.

Creating a Woman's Space 3 metrical cloud-like cushions of satiny fabric enclose them even in their Victorian dresses, which drape and curve. The reading figure is tethered into a dark enclosure by the fragmented lines of her shade, while the compositional lines of the windows and shades draw the sleeping figure further into the painting with long, sweeping movements. Egg emphasizes the significance of female companionship through her choice of subject matter and perspective on the female figure.

Despite the fact that one sister is sleeping and their communication is sluggish, they appear content in each other's company. The two companions' sharing of this small space and accompanying one another seems to emphasize their need for one another and their sympathetic relationship, despite the fact that this painting may highlight the differences between them— one dozing and more disheveled, and the other prim and diligently reading—and the separation of their activities. Additionally, because we are able to observe most of the carriage space from a close distance, we as viewers share their intimacy. In the Victorian social world, the small carriage car transforms into a focused, intimate, and feminine space.

In his 1864 painting Golden Hours, aesthetic painter Lord Frederick Leighton presents a bold yet subtle use of space and the positioning of the female figure. This painting is another vivid example of significantly charged female space. The female figure here faces the painting, which is unusual because it only shows the viewer her back. While he contemplatively plays the piano, she pays attention to the man who appears to be poetic. A charged, intimate space is created when her implied gaze and his downward glance meet in the center of the painting. Despite the fact that only her sleeve overlaps his, this center space is quiet, private, and intimate, even though the connection appears passionate. This mood is subtly reflected in the background, which shifts from dull to brighter gold across the canvas. Despite being depicted in a conventionally committed romantic relationship, this woman creates her own private space, excluding the painter and apparent voyeurs. We are simultaneously drawn into her experience by our intimate perspective. A determined decision and attitude are reflected in this composition, which emphasizes her reclamations of feminine and private space. She contributes actively to the painting's relationship and composition, directing an equal and intertwined energy toward her male companion. Egg's and Leighton's paintings depict women in typical Victorian settings and roles; However, the viewer is given a sense of the female figure and mind as a result of their choices for spatial composition, which can be interpreted as personal, assertive, and indicative of these women's inner lives and connections.

These two visual and art historical examples show how spaces and spatial compositions can be read for meaning. Already, reading spaces are being combined verbally and visually in the language. Michael Pollan observes that architects view their work as "a form of 'writing' rather than design," and he draws parallels between architecture and literature (Pollan 68–69). Textual and architectural 4 Spatial Dynamics and Female Development in Victorian Art and Novels conflate as personal, social, and symbolic meaning spaces. Daphne Spain extends this connection by claiming that the spatial design of buildings considers the ways in which individuals relate to society (Spain 7), focusing specifically on architectural spaces. Spain's concept of spatial structures as loci for social meanings and relationships seems to be easily extended to include other spaces and locations, even though she specifically refers to architecturally constructed spaces. The meaning of a space is written on it, and artists and writers write significance on the spaces they choose.

I will examine the way spatial composition works in a selection of Victorian novels written by women, particularly with regard to the development of female characters, using this art historical framework or lens:

Villette by Charlotte Brönte (1853), Wives and Daughters by Elizabeth Gaskell (1864–1866), and Middlemarch by George Eliot (1872) I've chosen these three novels because they focus on the domestic nature of women's spaces. I want to focus on how these women writers use space to show their gender. But outside the scope of this investigation, the spatial dynamics in these novels may also apply to other Victorian works. I intend to ask these texts the following specific questions in this study:

1. How do these Victorian women comment on their female characters using a visual language that constructs spatial composition and environment?

2. What is the spatial composition's response to the conditions and circumstances of the female characters?

3. Is there any correlation between female thought, imagination, creativity, etc. and spatial composition?

4. What role does this mix of visual and written elements play in the story?

I intend to investigate the connections and patterns that exist between these novels as well as their connection to visual art by asking these questions.

I argue that Victorian women's novels' spatial dynamics, as depicted in the art of the time, carry over into and exist in these Victorian novels, as well as being an aspect of the period to investigate. Lucy Snowe, the narrator of Villette, constructs both her narrative and her "self" through the use of spatial descriptions and representations. The protagonist of Gaskell, Molly Gibson, chooses and creates spaces in her home and community that help her develop her self-identity and broaden her social connections. The gradual inner growth of Dorothea Brooke from her initial inadequacies is symbolized by space metaphors in texts, architecture, rooms, artwork, and portraits from Creating a Woman's Space 5 Eliot. Through a literal and symbolic focus on spatial dynamics, the three authors allow their female protagonists to transcend Victorian womanly boundaries.

Anita Brookner, a contemporary British novelist and art historian, wrote Hotel du Lac (1984), which I will discuss briefly as an epilogue to this focused Victorian study. To see if these questions are relevant to a contemporary writer, particularly one who is frequently regarded as being directly influenced by the Victorians, when developing her female characters and responding to our current world seems provocative and potentially fruitful. I may be able to evaluate my questions and determine whether they transcend the Victorian era and its concerns by taking even a brief look at the work of a contemporary author who also pays close attention to spatial composition.

The inquiry into the connection between female imagination or thought and spatial representation appears to be at the project's center, based on these questions I pose to the texts. In the novels of these authors, the interaction of the visual and verbal creates crucial spaces for women that encourage individual growth, creative possibilities, and potential growth. As part of the authors' strategies for developing and expanding their primary female characters, the visual depictions of space surrounding these female characters are unique to them. (Mairs 110–11) Nancy Mairs acknowledges a significant connection between her gender, personal spaces, and language use. Her relationship with femaleness and space is intimate, familiar, and productive. I find this kind of relationship in the novels written by Victorian women authors and these depictions of Victorian women.

Recent research on female development in literature intersects with my perception of space as a realm of possibilities and the nature of space itself.

"The way to womanhood not as a single path to a clear destination but as the endless negotiation of a crossroads," Susan Fraiman writes. Women take distinct paths that constantly change to reflect their individuality (Fraiman x). The way Fraiman approaches women in the novel of development suggests that women's narratives are valued for their inherent possibilities and alternatives. As a result, focusing on the artistic and narrative applications of spatial composition to open up these possibilities seems especially appropriate.

My research design initially employs art historical methodology in light of the study's joint focus on literature and art. According to Erwin Panofsky's 1955 book Meanings in the Visual Arts, I will first analyze my chosen works of art using an iconographical method. This approach is broken down by Panofsky into a pre-iconographical description and an iconographical analysis. The final step, which Panofsky calls "iconology," then looks at trends, cultural context, literary correlations, 6 Spatial Dynamics and Female Development in Victorian Art and Novels, and other things. When looking into the symbolism and spatial dynamics of these Victorian works, it seems that this method of reading the iconography of the painting and connecting it to a cultural context is a good one. Using Rosalind Krauss' 1977 book Passages in Modern Sculpture as an example, I will sharpen this method by looking at how form structure affects meaning.

I also want to incorporate a cultural or poststructuralist

approach into my method, as Griselda Pollock, an art historian, does. Gender and power, which underlie most artistic decisions, will be addressed in this post-structuralist foray into semiotics and signification.

My approach to literature will also be guided by these painting methods. To put it another way, I intend to give close readings of the books (or the parts of the books that are most closely related to the female protagonists) using a cultural/feminist approach and semiotic consideration of the significance of signs to find a Victorian context for the roles, domestic life, and positions played by women in the books.

As artistic responses to Victorian society, gender representations, and locations of resonant symbols, this parallel research design enables valid connections between literature and art to emerge and be discussed on a common plain.

This project promises to improve our understanding of

women's self-perceptions in the nineteenth century and to aid in the ongoing process of decoding representations of women that are relevant to both the nineteenth and twentieth centuries. This project involves communication between two distinct discourses because it will take a visually-oriented approach to three Victorian women writers and their works; It will recognize and make use of the connections that existed between novels and paintings by combining literary criticism with approaches to art history. This kind of intertextuality has only been looked at in novels in previous research. However, I want to focus instead on the ways that novels and paintings appear to speak the same language; Consequently, I anticipate that this project will contribute to the ongoing reevaluation of generic boundaries.

Chapter One: Doors to the imaginations and worlds of women:

Victorian Art's Visual Female Spaces Space that has been seized by the imagination cannot remain indifferent to the surveyor's measurements and estimates. It has been lived in, but not in a positive way but with all of the imagination's bias.

—Gaston Bachelard, The Poetics of Space (xxxii). According to Bachelard, people claim and make their own spaces. Regardless of the length of time that passes since the initial contact or period of residence, the space no longer remains empty. Instead, it transforms into the focal point or positon of personal claim, imagination, and thought. A place often carries a sense of one's own identity, or something of one's essence. In the end, that personal presence adds some weight to the space. This is a constant flow of movement and energy in life. That charge is temporarily held in some places; People we spend more time with become more crowded and intimate.

It's possible that this description gives the

impression of being rather philosophical and speculative, or that it gives the impression that it doesn't need to be said. One's general level of depth of observation and connection to one's surroundings are likely related to one's perception.

However, for a lot of artists, how they perceive space and the unique dynamics of it are crucial to the composition, life, and meaning of their work. Rosalind Krauss compares the emergence of energy from a central space to the concentric age rings on a tree trunk in her writing about how space is essential to the organic nature of contemporary three-dimensional art (Krauss 253). The arrangement of pictorial shapes, lines, and color, light, and value blocks is another aspect of spatial composition. A two-dimensional, pictorial surface can provide a sense of space by constantly shifting perspective and depth. As the shapes and forms become recognizable entities—the material, the natural, and the human—space becomes an even more important and vitalizing   8 Spatial Dynamics and Female Development in Victorian Art and Novels force beyond those common organizational functions. Space is now a part of meaning, definition, and, most importantly, possibility.

Artwork from any era can, of course, benefit from this description of space's dynamics. It works in the same way for everyone; The particulars are located in the meanings that emerge. Therefore, it follows that Victorian art, perhaps best known for its intricate, three-dimensional, or illusionistic imagery and symbolism, would use spatial composition to convey meaning. This way, Victorian paintings' visual elements suggest literal ways to interpret individual meanings in their compositions. I want to examine the ways that spatial composition and dynamics suggest meaning, particularly for the female figure, in this section and throughout the study as a whole. The spaces women occupy and inhabit in these paintings may hold, as Bachelard describes, elements of their energy and imaginations, in addition to depicting certain Victorian living conditions and aspects of the social and psychological milieu of the time.

In general, Victorian art from the middle of the 1800s to the latter decades of the century lacks a unified style, goal, or movement. Instead, multiple movements with varying levels of social esteem and artistic inspiration existed simultaneously. The group of artists known as the Pre-Raphaelites emerged around the middle of the 20th century. Throughout their existence, the group of artists experimented with various sources of inspiration and influenced. In essence, the artists of this movement are well-known for their close observation of nature, the profound influence of the artist and social critic John Ruskin, and their depiction of scenes and rendering of form inspired by literature and legends from the Middle Ages, Arthurian times, and Shakespeare. The group as a whole is regarded as imaginative and observational artists. The aesthetic and Victorian Renaissance artists frequently depicted characters or events from Roman or Greek mythology in their works, with a focus on classical themes, forms, moods, and styles. While a number of artists from this era were also Academy members, the styles of others suggested a cautious transition into modernism. The Academic/Social painters showed familiar scenes of Victorian life, either in the home or in society as a whole, as depicted in a traditional way. Each group responded to and commented on their society and time, regardless of movement or style. These very different artists frequently exhibited together, blending their methods and artistic responses for the audience.

I selected works from this extensive and diverse group of artists and works of art for this study. The first thing I did was narrow my choices down to pictures of women in close proximity to one another or their surroundings. Although every painting uses space in its composition, I tried to choose works in which space appeared to be the most important organizational or stylistic element in Windows to Women's Worlds, Portals to their Imaginations 9. I chose paintings that either emphasized typical domestic spaces or opened creative or imaginative possibilities for women within this format, keeping in mind that the purpose of this visual survey is to eventually draw comparisons and connections to several women's novels of the time. In addition, the artists represented in this selection are not all male or female. Even though the connections will only be made to female novelists, it would seem unbalanced and incomplete to exclude artists of either gender. The majority of the period's well-studied and familiar images were created by male artists, who dominated the scene at the time. Similar to efforts made by female writers at the time, professional Victorian female artists just struggled to become recognized and accepted members of the artistic community; Their works are crucial for both completing the overall perceptions of women in the nineteenth century and identifying any variations in how women are depicted according to their gender. I want this group of paintings to not only serve as a microcosm of the art of the time, but also to highlight the artistic recognition that space can serve as a visual correlate for the female mind and imagination.

I have categorized these selected works into distinct groups in order to impose some sort of order on them. There is no restriction on these groups. In fact, as I chose where to put myself, I found that there were a lot of areas that overlapped, shared elements, and possibilities for interpretation. However, in order to provide some direction for the analysis, these groups focus on a common, underlying theme that permeates the works. I'll start by looking at paintings that show women in domestic, typically enclosed, interior settings. Then, I'll look at women who were placed in a few typical Victorian outdoor settings, most of which were extensions of the home. The next group will focus on women who are creatively involved in artistic settings. Last but not least, I'll consider the implications of women in "symbolic" spaces. In light of this progression, it is interesting to note that all of the spaces, not just the "fantasy" or more unconventional compositions of the previous group, take on symbolic significance.

Before getting into the specific images, I want to mention the essay "Modernity and the Spaces of Femininity" by art critic and historian Griselda Pollock as a general consideration for the gendered choice of spaces. Pollock inquires as to whether male and female artists choose the same locations for their scenes. She first thinks of "spaces" as places. She says that female impressionists tend to place their subjects in private spaces, such as the home.1 When female impressionists do venture into public spaces, these spaces are places of "bourgeois recreation," like the beach or a park, or the scenes show working-class women working for a bourgeois household (Pollock, Vision 56). In the meantime, Pollock draws attention to the male impressionists who frequent and portray public spaces like bars, cafes, backstages, and streets 10 Spatial Dynamics and Female Development in Victorian Art and Novels. She describes these areas as "socially fluid" When determining the positions of the subject, the artist, and the viewer, Pollock simultaneously takes into consideration the painting's spatial order or structure—angles of vision, framing devices, boundaries, and compression of space" (62–63). She then suggests a phenomenology of space that gives the positioning meaning and value; Instead of being represented abstractly, space is shown with senses Different inflections of response and relationships to social processes are made possible by these sensory and visual cues (65–66).

Printed in Great Britain
by Amazon

19022326R00037